Willard Hotel

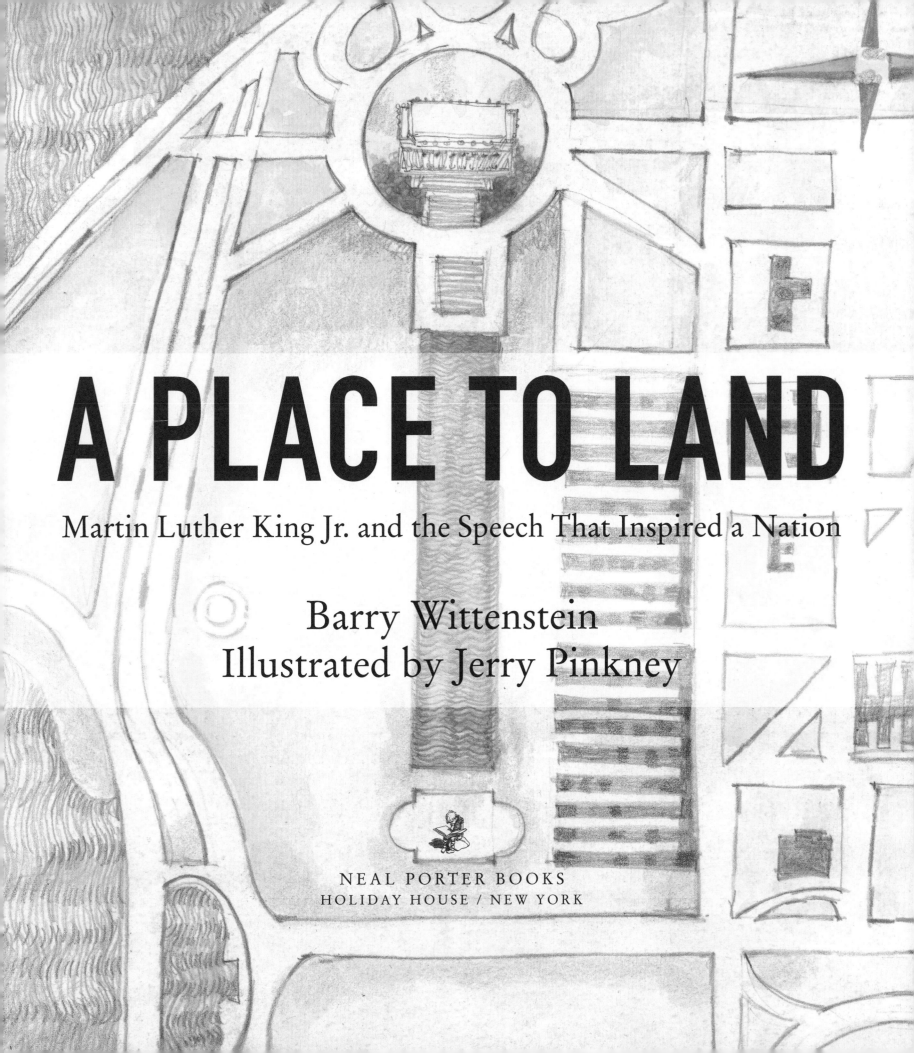

A PLACE TO LAND

Martin Luther King Jr. and the Speech That Inspired a Nation

Barry Wittenstein
Illustrated by Jerry Pinkney

NEAL PORTER BOOKS
HOLIDAY HOUSE / NEW YORK

Martin Luther King Jr.

was once asked if the hardest part
of preaching was knowing where to begin.

"No," he said.

"The hardest part is knowing where to end.

"It's terrible to be circling up there
without a place to land."

But on August 27th,
the night before the 1963 March on Washington,
the strong and steady voice of the civil rights movement
wasn't sure what to say, or how to say it.

So Martin did what great men do.
He asked for guidance.
Not from above.
At least, not at first.

In the lobby of the Willard Hotel
where Abraham Lincoln once stood,
a meeting of the minds took place.

"You have to preach," said Reverend Ralph Abernathy. "Most of the folks coming tomorrow are coming to hear you preach."

Wyatt Tee Walker agreed, but added, "Don't use the lines about 'I have a dream.' You have used it too many times already."

Bayard Rustin, who organized the march, wanted to hear about jobs, jobs, and more jobs, not dreams or Scripture.

Clarence Jones,
one of Martin's speechwriters
(yes, even Martin had speechwriters!),
suggested a marvelous metaphor,
a fresh metaphor,
one never heard before:

"A bad check."

It meant
the time had come for America
to make good on her promise of equality
and pay up,
for her citizens of color had grown weary,
frustrated, and angry
for justice long overdue.

Reverend Walter Fauntroy agreed.
"Whatever you do," he said, "keep that in there."

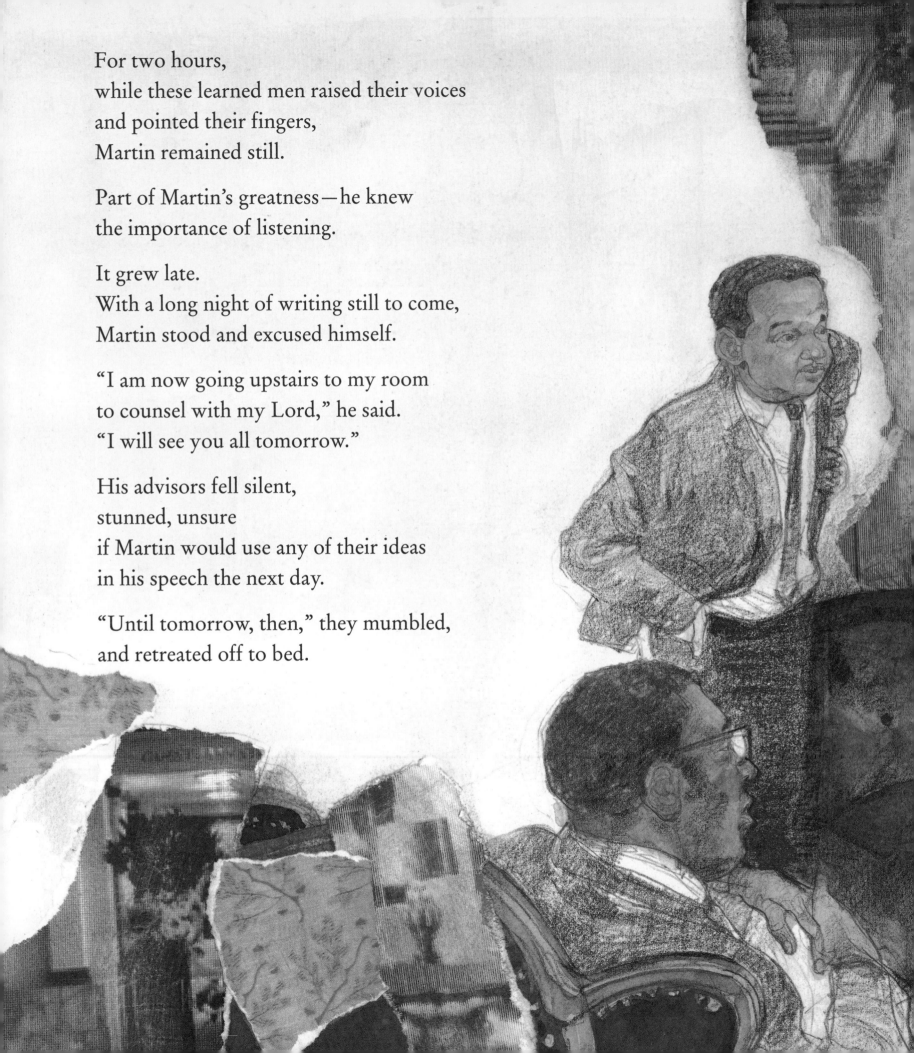

For two hours,
while these learned men raised their voices
and pointed their fingers,
Martin remained still.

Part of Martin's greatness—he knew
the importance of listening.

It grew late.
With a long night of writing still to come,
Martin stood and excused himself.

"I am now going upstairs to my room
to counsel with my Lord," he said.
"I will see you all tomorrow."

His advisors fell silent,
stunned, unsure
if Martin would use any of their ideas
in his speech the next day.

"Until tomorrow, then," they mumbled,
and retreated off to bed.

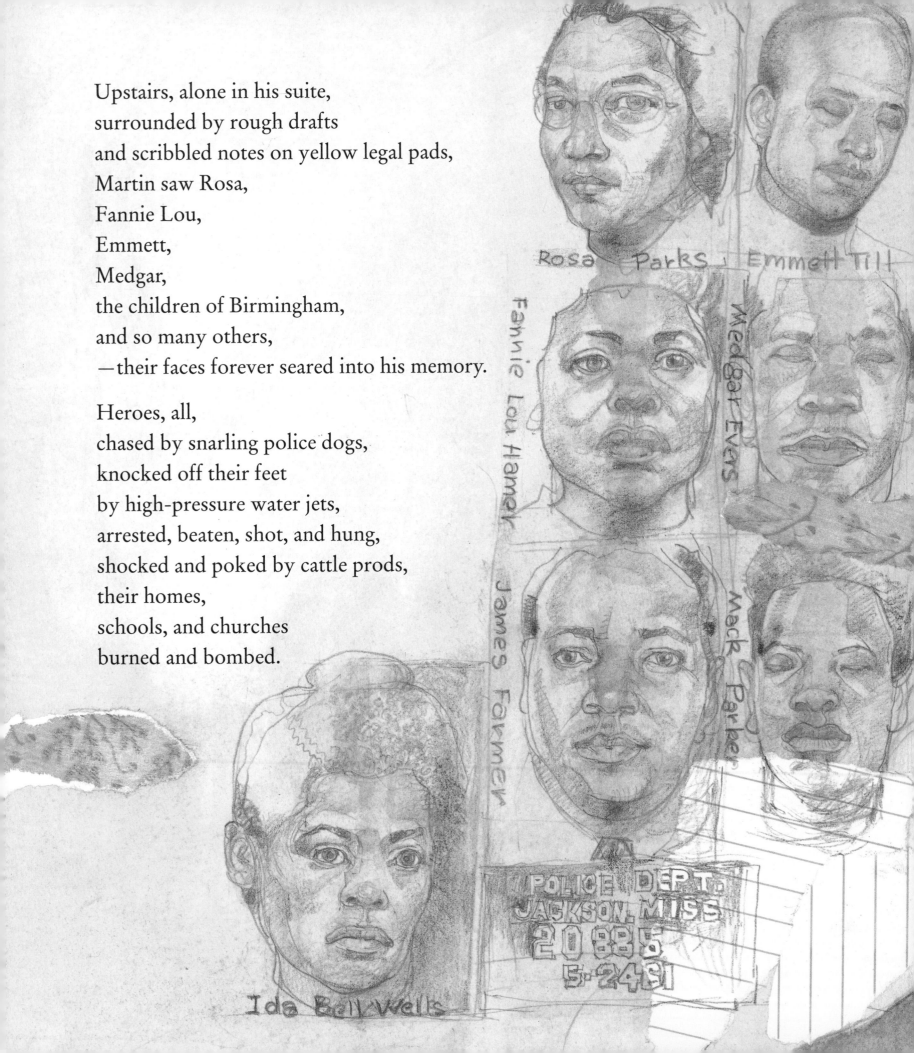

Upstairs, alone in his suite,
surrounded by rough drafts
and scribbled notes on yellow legal pads,
Martin saw Rosa,
Fannie Lou,
Emmett,
Medgar,
the children of Birmingham,
and so many others,
—their faces forever seared into his memory.

Heroes, all,
chased by snarling police dogs,
knocked off their feet
by high-pressure water jets,
arrested, beaten, shot, and hung,
shocked and poked by cattle prods,
their homes,
schools, and churches
burned and bombed.

Diane Nash

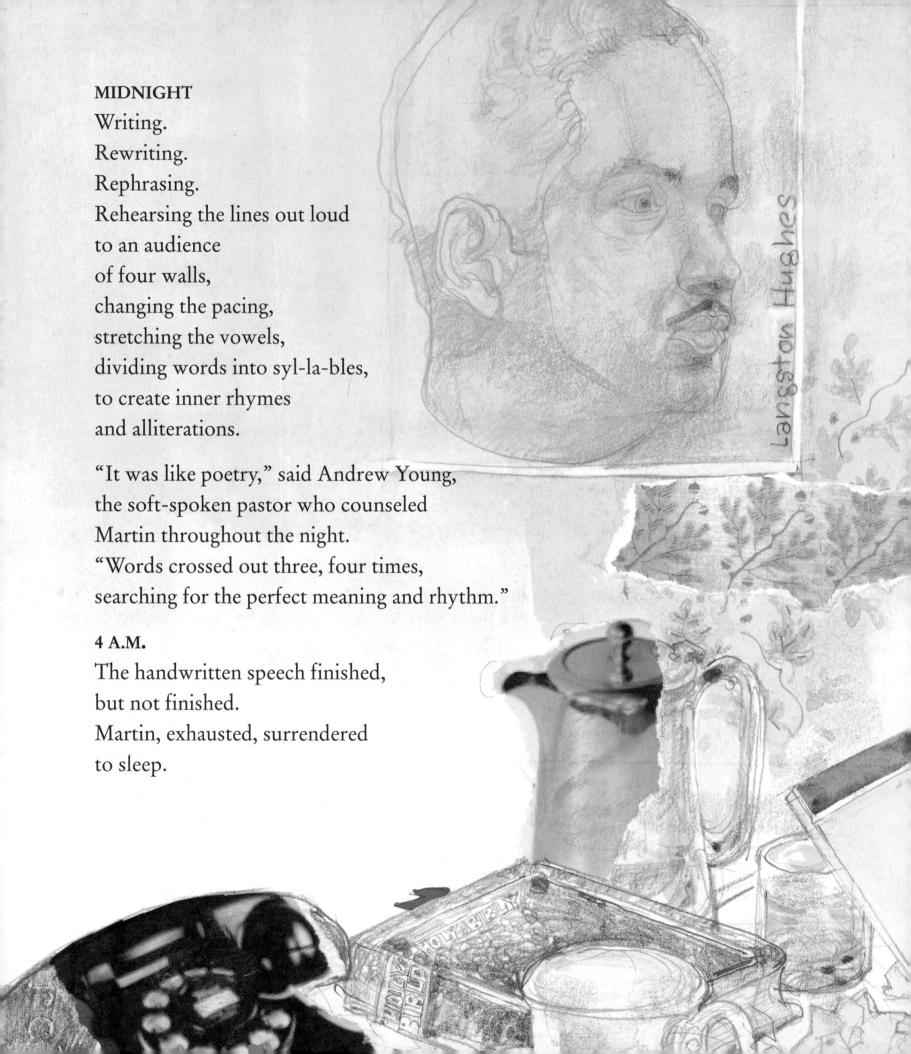

MIDNIGHT
Writing.
Rewriting.
Rephrasing.
Rehearsing the lines out loud
to an audience
of four walls,
changing the pacing,
stretching the vowels,
dividing words into syl-la-bles,
to create inner rhymes
and alliterations.

"It was like poetry," said Andrew Young,
the soft-spoken pastor who counseled
Martin throughout the night.
"Words crossed out three, four times,
searching for the perfect meaning and rhythm."

4 A.M.
The handwritten speech finished,
but not finished.
Martin, exhausted, surrendered
to sleep.

Langston Hughes

Andrew Young

While at the same time,
up in Harlem in New York City,
on 125th Street,
in Chicago and Philadelphia,
Cleveland and Memphis,
crowds cheered friends and relatives
climbing aboard chartered buses and trains,
on foot and on planes,
singing "We Shall Overcome."

8 A.M.

Hoping for a peaceful day,
the shining city on the Potomac
awoke to armed soldiers
patrolling Constitution Avenue,
as if preparing for war
against an invading army.

NOON
Women in flowing white dresses,
gentlemen in pressed white shirts
and snazzy fedoras,
carrying signs of protest,
carrying signs of hope,
walked past the Reflecting Pool,
watching their reflections silhouetted
against the bluest of pearl blue skies.

2:30 P.M.
Martin kept refining:
Painting with a preacher's fine brush,
a light shade of wisdom here,
a darker shade of frustration there,
the darkest shade of "for whites only"
everywhere.

APPROACHING 3:30 P.M.

Introduced as "the moral leader of our nation,"
Martin stood at the podium,
ready to lead his people to the Promised Land.

He removed the folded white sheet of paper
from the pocket of his black suit,
the speech typed and finished,
but never finished,
and placed it flat onto the lectern.

Under the watchful, marble eyes
of the sixteenth president, Abraham Lincoln,
Martin's rich baritone,
—God's trombone—
rang out across the ages,
gathering the glorious images
of the Constitution,
the Declaration of Independence,
the Emancipation Proclamation,
and wrapping them around the writings
of Langston Hughes,
the Bible,
and spirituals
he learned as a child.

Adding a sentence for emphasis,
replacing a word for clarity,
changes made
in the moment
to match the mood
of the moment.

The speech was good.
The crowd applauded where it should.
But Martin wanted more.

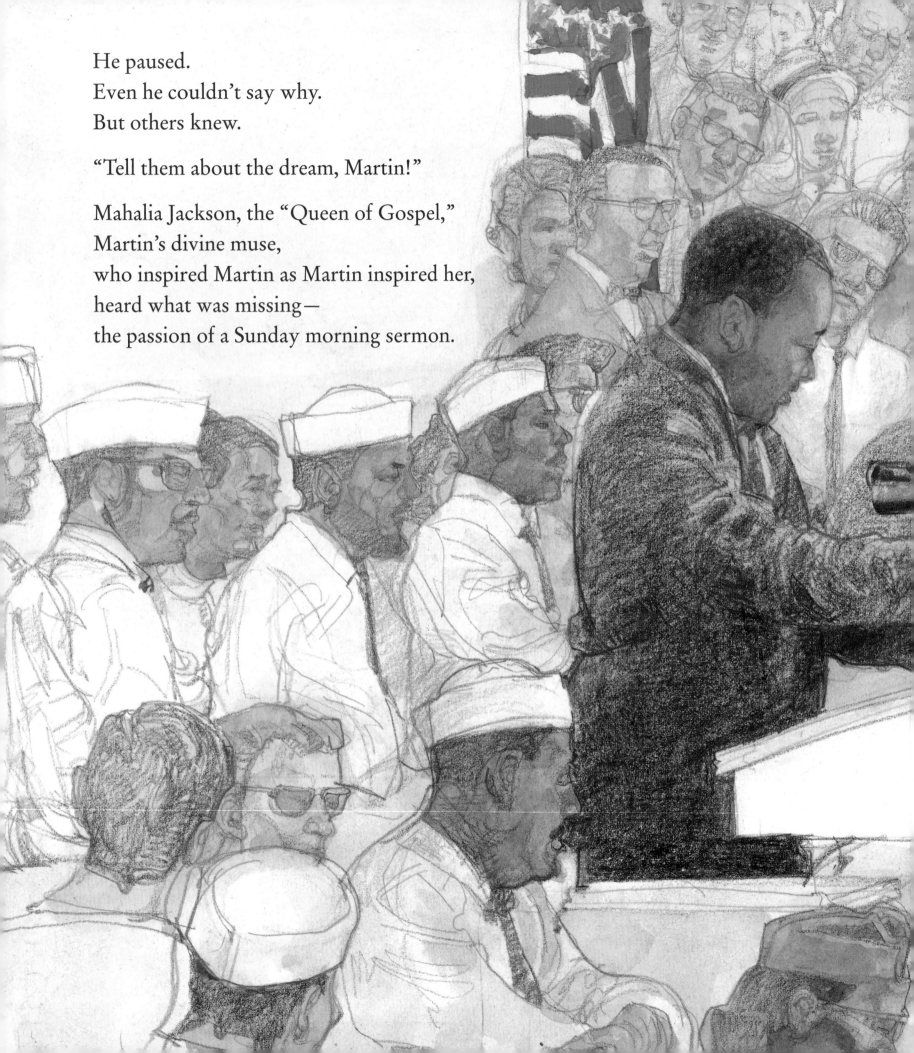

He paused.
Even he couldn't say why.
But others knew.

"Tell them about the dream, Martin!"

Mahalia Jackson, the "Queen of Gospel,"
Martin's divine muse,
who inspired Martin as Martin inspired her,
heard what was missing—
the passion of a Sunday morning sermon.

Again, she shouted,
"Tell them about the dream,
Martin! Tell them about the dream!"

The Baptist preacher,
son, grandson, and great-grandson of Baptist preachers,
carefully moved the script off to the side.

Martin was done circling.
The lecture was over.
He was going to church,
his place to land,
and taking a congregation
of two hundred and fifty thousand
along for the ride.

Reverend Martin Luther King Sr.

Reverend Adam Daniel Williams

Four words
spoken many times,
in Chicago; Detroit; Birmingham;
and Albany, Georgia,
but never as emotional
as on this day,
never intended to be heard
on this day,
not even written down
for this day.
Not even once!

I HAVE

A DREAM.

Words he risked his life for,
and spent time in jail for,
to convince black America
and white America
that walking arm in arm
was the only way
to save America.

Martin's voice soared as sweetly as Mahalia's,
from "My country 'tis of thee" to
"Let freedom ring!"
concluding with the mighty crescendo,
"Free at last! Free at last!
Thank God Almighty, we are free at last!"

Through the crowd,
and from sea to shining sea,
tears rolled down like a mighty stream,
because the vision of a world
where love triumphs over hate
grabs hold of the heart and won't let go.
This was the picture Martin painted.
This was his gift,
further proof of his greatness.

But now was not the time for congratulations.
There was one more stop to make.

4 P.M.
Whisked away to the White House,
a house built by those enslaved,
to meet the thirty-fifth president,
John F. Kennedy,
who had been slow to embrace the civil rights movement,
and tried to convince its leaders to cancel the march,
now greeted those same men into the Oval Office,
extending a handshake to all,
but saving a special welcome for Martin:
"I have a dream."

For some in the room,
Kennedy's warm smile and handshake
were bittersweet.

8 P.M.

Returning to the Willard Hotel
where less than twenty-four hours earlier,
voices were raised
and fingers were pointed,
the wise men gathered once again,
this time to celebrate,
and to reflect upon the day that was.

"Leader, you swept today," Reverend Abernathy
told Martin.
"You preached today," John Lewis added.
"You was smoking,"
Clarence Jones had told Martin
moments after the speech.
"The words were so hot
they was just burning off the page."

A. Philip Randolph

John Lewis

A. Philip Randolph

They all knew more battles lay ahead—
angry late-night meetings in hotel lobbies,
frantic phone calls,
tears and blood to be shed,
fighting every inch to cross a bridge
to make Martin's dream come true.

And those battles continue to be fought.

But that night brought optimism and laughter,
for they all agreed.

Martin stepped up to the lectern,
and stepped down on the other side
of history.

Shirley Chisholm, Congress

John Lewis, Congress

President Barack Obama

THE Civil Rights Act of 1964

Eighty-eighth Con...

...ted States of Ame...

A Note from the Author

Martin Luther King Jr. arrived in Washington, D.C., on August 27, 1963, the evening before the March on Washington. His speech the next day would be heard by 250,000 in attendance, and broadcast to millions around the world.

After months of organizing the massive event, agonizing over details, there was just one issue left to resolve.

The speech.

It was not yet finished. In fact, no final words had been put to paper.

For good reason.

The speech was a tightrope King had to navigate if the march was to be successful. It needed to present a compelling and convincing argument for the end of segregation, and had to put the need for integration in a historical, moral, and patriotic context. Plus, it had to speak to a number of disparate groups, each of whom had its own agenda.

Is there any wonder Martin was not settled on what to say, or what tone to use to say it?

Still, what confidence Dr. King must have had in his own intellectual and writing ability—and those of his advisors—to put himself in such a situation the night before.

For Dr. King and the civil rights movement, it had been an incredibly busy, and violent, year.

In the spring and early summer, Dr. King had gone to Birmingham, Alabama, to help integrate one of the most racially segregated cities in the South. He was jailed for eight days, during which his scribbled notes were smuggled out by his attorney, Dr. Clarence B. Jones. These notes would eventually be published as "Letter from Birmingham Jail."

But Dr. King's efforts weren't making any headway until the police department, under the direction of Eugene "Bull" Connor, decided to use attack dogs and high-pressure water hoses against young protestors. Thanks to Connor's brutal actions, many white Americans saw images on their televisions for the first time of the nation's racial unrest, shocking even President Kennedy.

Then in June, shortly after Birmingham, civil rights activist Medgar Evers was shot and killed in his own driveway.

While all this was happening, Dr. King was putting the finishing touches on his book *Why We Can't Wait* and trying to find time to spend with his wife and children.

Finally, on Saturday, August 24, four days before he would deliver the speech of his life, Dr. King sat down in Clarence Jones's apartment in Riverdale, New York, with a rough draft written by Jones and fellow speechwriter, Stanley Levison.

Two days later, Dr. King flew down to Atlanta and continued editing the speech with Ed Clayton, a colleague with the Southern Christian Leadership Conference. The working title was "Normalcy—Never Again." (At some point, there was an edit of this, so there are actually two "Normalcy—Never Again" speeches.)

On Tuesday, the day before the March on Washington, Dr. King flew there. Later that evening, he met in the lobby of the Willard Hotel with nine of his closest advisors. (Why in the lobby? Their rooms were surely bugged by the FBI.)

Into the night, after retiring to his suite, Dr. King took sections of all the versions and edited them together to make them his own. One crucial piece was Clarence Jones's "bad check" metaphor from the previous Saturday night's draft. Martin loved it.

There are conflicting accounts whether Martin ever

considered featuring his "I Have a Dream" theme. A young man in the hotel room next to Martin's says he heard Dr. King practicing the famous words. Others, like Dr. Jones, don't think it was ever in his mind to either replace "bad check" or to use both metaphors.

It was hot in Washington on August 28. Many in the crowd were exhausted from their all-night sojourns, and faced equally long return trips home.

With the exception of young John Lewis, the chairman of the Student Nonviolent Coordinating Committee, who invigorated the crowd with his fiery words, most of the speeches elicited little reaction.

People began to depart for home.

Then Martin, the last speaker, took the podium. Reading from his prepared remarks, he sounded more university professor than preacher.

Suddenly, ten minutes in, he went off script, improvising the last seven minutes of his speech into what we now know as "I Have a Dream." What made him switch gears?

Apparently—as speechwriter Clarence Jones confirms—Mahalia Jackson shouted to King, encouraging him to talk like a preacher. While Dr. King's powerful preaching and oratory skills were well known to the African American community, they were largely unknown and unheard by white America. Mahalia knew it was this straight-from-the-heart emotion that was missing.

King knew it, too.

However, the "improvising" was not exactly one hundred percent improvised. As it turns out, the "I have a dream" repeating stanzas were one of Dr. King's "set pieces." It was a memorized piece that Martin would tailor to whatever audience and situation he was preaching to. "Free at last" was another set-piece used by Martin that day.

Within weeks, several record companies released Martin's performance of this untitled speech. Dr. Jones, an attorney, soon filed a copyright notice to restrict its dissemination.

However, when he was filing the proper paperwork, Jones didn't know what to name it. Martin had not given it a title. It was Jones who decided to call it "I Have a Dream." In retrospect, it seems like an obvious decision. But imagine if Jones had copyrighted it as "Bad Check." Would history have embraced it?

For five years after the march, Malcolm X and Stokely Carmichael attempted to marginalize Dr. King. These newer voices dismissed Dr. King's vision of an integrated society, instead promoting the idea of separation.

Malcolm X's comment that Dr. King's dream would become a "nightmare" came true just three weeks later, in September 1963, when the 16th Street Baptist Church in Birmingham, Alabama, was bombed, killing four young girls. Years later, to his disappointment, Dr. King agreed with Malcolm X's assessment.

Today, however, the words "I Have a Dream" have travelled around the world, across generations, and given hope to all who are oppressed.

—B.W.

A Note from the Artist

I began *A Place to Land* with great interest in the subject—civil rights generally, and Dr. Martin Luther King Jr. specifically. The text, by Barry Wittenstein, struck me as both powerful and nuanced, expressing King's strength as well as his vulnerabilities, his sureness and concerns, his resolve and patience, his role as listener and conduit. Having honed my craft in book-making for well over fifty years, I was certainly up to the task of visualizing and interpreting Barry's manuscript.

But there was a deeper connection too. I played my own small role in the push for social justice as a member of the Boston Action Group in the early 1960s. We focused on getting African Americans out to vote and advocated for equal opportunities for decent work and fair wages. I can still vividly recall those times, sitting together late into the night and listening to civil rights activists returning from the contentious South. I found their experiences of marching and demonstrating in a hostile landscape riveting, and I was deeply inspired by the energy and courage of those soldiers who believed in putting it all on the line.

Twice now I have had the privilege of being challenged to create images honoring the legacy of Dr. Martin Luther King Jr. The first was in 1979, when I designed the United States Postal Service Black Heritage Stamp commemorating MLK's life and courage. *A Place to Land* gave me an opportunity to go even deeper. In his "I Have a Dream" speech, King had the audacity of aligning himself with the U.S. Constitution, which states that all men are created equal. My task was to dramatize King's process in drafting his remarks for that all-important hot day in August 1963, that historic touchstone in our country's struggle to remain true to its foundation. I felt a heightened enthusiasm for how I could make my artistic practice do justice to such a monumental figure and such a potent time in American history.

With exhaustive—oftentimes dizzying—research, I gathered materials, acquiring a *Hip Pocket Guide of The United States Constitution: What It Says, What It Means*, reading articles and personal accounts, and sifting through hundreds of images. With so many sources, I knew early on that I would use collage as a way to reinforce place. Yet I also wanted my art to capture MLK as a living idea: articulate and poetic orator, truth-teller, witness to this nation's injustices, and beacon of hope. Eventually, I came across a compelling and arresting photograph of the successful crossing of the Edmund Pettus Bridge in 1965. The first effort, on March 7, had ended in the infamous Bloody Sunday, where hundreds of protestors were beaten by police at the bridge on their way from Selma to Montgomery. On March 21, they finally made it across, and the photograph shows King on the front lines with demonstrators, all of them wearing Hawaiian leis, a symbol of love. Even though it took place nearly two years after the Dream speech, this iconic image gave me my starting point—the "bridge" in my image-making—to illustrate King's journey from Baptist preacher to civil rights spearhead.

To this day, King's legacy encourages us to look inward to face our flaws, and outward to join in his mission of peace, shaping our future in the journey toward equality. One can still visit those historic sites—the lobby of the Willard InterContinental Hotel, the National Mall, and the Lincoln Memorial, where 250,000 peaceful women, men, and children, both white and black, gathered, clapped, and shed tears of joy as Dr. Martin Luther King Jr. delivered his powerfully resonant words: "I have a dream."

—J.P.

The Willard Hotel Advisors

Reverend Ralph Abernathy (1926–1990) was a Baptist minister, who with Dr. King organized the historic Montgomery Bus Boycott. He cofounded the Southern Christian Leadership Conference (SCLC). He is considered a major civil rights figure, serving as close advisor to Dr. King. He was also Martin's closest friend. After Dr. King's assassination, Abernathy became the president of the SCLC.

Reverend Walter Fauntroy (1933–) was the director of the Washington Bureau of the Southern Christian Leadership Conference, and served as D.C. Coordinator of the historic March on Washington for Jobs and Freedom. Fauntroy was also coordinator for the 1965 Selma-to-Montgomery March for voting rights and the 1966 Meredith Mississippi March Against Fear. In 1966, President Lyndon Johnson appointed him Vice Chairman of the White House Conference on Civil Rights. In 1967 he became Vice Chairman of the D.C. City Council.

Clarence B. Jones (1931–) was a former personal counsel, advisor, draft speechwriter, and close friend of Dr. King's. It was his suggestion to use the "bad check" metaphor, which Dr. King did. Jones was one of the nine men who met with Dr. King at the Willard Hotel on August 27, 1963, to advise on the content of his speech. Jones is currently a Scholar in Residence at the Martin Luther King, Jr. Research and Education Institute at Stanford University.

Reverend Bernard Lee (1935–1991) was a civil rights advocate, a vice president of the Southern Christian Leadership Conference, and a founding member of the 1960 Student Nonviolent Coordinating Committee. He marched with his close friend Dr. King from Selma to Montgomery in 1965.

Professor Lawrence Reddick (1910–1995) was a historian, author, and Harvard (among other institutions) professor interested in racist depictions of African Americans in popular culture. While teaching at Alabama State College in Montgomery at the height of the bus boycott in 1955, he met Dr. King. Reddick subsequently travelled with King to India in 1959 to deepen their understanding of Gandhian principles of nonviolent social change and to Oslo, Norway, in 1964, when King received the Nobel Peace Prize.

Cleveland Robinson (1916–1995) was an important American labor organizer and key civil rights activist. He was Chairman of the Administrative Committee for the March on Washington. Based in New York City, he worked hard to get minority representation in various labor unions. In 1990, he helped organize Nelson Mandela's first visit to New York.

Bayard Rustin (1912–1987) was in charge of the immense job of organizing the march. As a student of Mahatma Gandhi's teachings, Rustin helped mold Martin Luther King Jr. into a worldwide icon of peace and nonviolence. Despite these achievements, Rustin was beaten, imprisoned, and dismissed from important positions of leadership because he lived as an openly gay man in an era of homophobia.

Wyatt Tee Walker (1928–2018) was an African American pastor, national civil rights leader, theologian, and cultural historian. Dr. Walker became one of the first board members of the Southern Christian Leadership Conference (SCLC) in 1958. That same year, he helped found a chapter of the Congress of Racial Equality. Between 1960 and 1964, Dr. Walker served as executive director of the SCLC, helping to bring the organization to prominence.

Andrew Young (1932–) visited Dr. King in his suite during the evening of August 27 to provide advice and to act as a sounding board. A pastor in his own right, Young joined the Southern Christian Leadership Conference (SCLC) in 1961. A trusted and close advisor to Dr. King, he was a thoughtful strategist for some of the most important protests, including the Birmingham campaign and the March on Washington. Young was the executive director of the SCLC between 1964 and 1968. He was instrumental in drafting the Civil Rights Act of 1964 and the Voting Rights Act of 1965. After the assassination of Dr. King, Young was named executive vice president of the SCLC (1968–1970).

Other Voices

Ed Clayton (1921–1966) was an author, editor, and journalist, as well as the public relations director of Dr. King's Southern Christian Leadership Council. Clayton and Dr. King worked on a draft of the speech two days before the March on Washington. He is one of the possible authors of one of the two "Normalcy—Never Again" working drafts.

Langston Hughes (1902–1967) was an American poet, social activist, novelist, playwright, and columnist. Hughes was an important literary figure during the 1920s, a period known as the "Harlem Renaissance." His writing portrayed the lives of the working-class blacks in America. Hughes's poetry is thought to have greatly influenced Dr. King's oratory. Scholars note the similarity between Hughes's "I Dream a World" poem and King's "I Have a Dream" speech.

Mahalia Jackson (1911–1972) was quoted by Clarence Jones and Ted Kennedy as having shouted to Dr. King, "Tell them about the dream, Martin! Tell them about the dream!" at the march. Jackson is considered one of the greatest musical figures in U.S. history. Closely associated for the last decade with the civil rights movement, Miss Jackson sang two songs at the March on Washington. She also sang at Dr. King's funeral in 1968.

Stanley Levison (1912–1979) was an attorney from New York and a lifelong activist in progressive causes. As a close friend and advisor to Dr. King, with Clarence Jones he helped write speeches, raise funds, and organize events. Because of his work with the Communist Party, Levison withdrew from his association with King, fearing staining the reputation of the civil rights movement and retribution from the FBI. He was a vitally important advisor, whose contributions have gone largely unnoticed.

Who Spoke at the March on Washington

The event began with a rally at the Washington Monument featuring many well-known speakers, including **Josephine Baker** (1906–1975), the famous actress and civil rights activist. The marchers then moved to the Lincoln Memorial, where the national anthem was sung, followed by speakers from various civil rights groups and organizations.

(1) Rev. Patrick O'Boyle (1896–1987), Archbishop of Washington, gave the invocation. He was a strong supporter of the use of nonviolence in the fight for civil rights. He had objected to some of the language in the advance copy of John Lewis's speech. The twenty-three-year-old Lewis, chairman of the Student Nonviolent Coordinating Committee, at first refused to rewrite certain parts of his speech. O'Boyle threatened to boycott the invocation unless Lewis acquiesced. Eventually, with the encouragement of A. Philip Randolph and others, Lewis agreed to tone down the rhetoric.

(2) A. Philip Randolph (1889–1979) was the elder statesman and head of the march. A leading voice in the labor movement, Randolph won a huge victory for the predominantly black workforce when he organized the Brotherhood of Sleeping Car Porters in 1925. In 1941, Randolph organized the first March on Washington movement to pressure President Franklin Roosevelt to issue Executive Order 8802, banning discrimination in defense industries. That march was called off when FDR agreed to do so.

(3) Dr. Eugene Carson Blake (1906–1985) was president of the National Council of Churches in the United States from 1954 to 1957. From 1951 to 1966, Blake served as the stated clerk of the United Presbyterian Church General Assembly. Blake was a strong critic of racial segregation who worked hard for peace and civil rights.

(4) Daisy Bates (1914–1999) was an American civil rights activist, publisher, and journalist who played a major role in the Little Rock Integration Crisis of 1957. Myrlie Evers, wife of Medgar Evers, was originally scheduled to speak, but missed her flight. The "Negro Women Fighters for Freedom" ceremony honored Ms. Bates, Diane Nash, Myrlie Evers, Mrs. Herbert Lee, Rosa Parks, and Gloria Richardson.

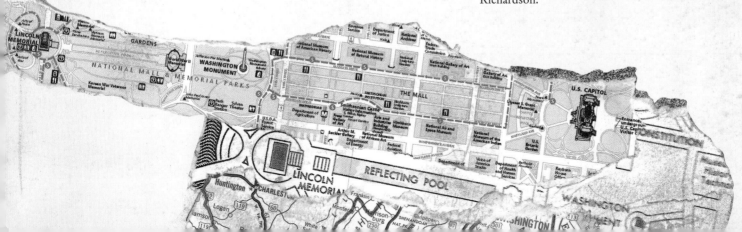

(5) **John Lewis** (1940–) was the youngest of all the speakers, and the twenty-three-year-old chairman of the Student Nonviolent Coordinating Committee. The strong language of the advance copy of his speech caused concern among the other leaders and Rev. Patrick O'Boyle. Lewis finally acquiesced to toning it down. Since 1987, as a United States representative from Georgia, John Lewis's voice continues to advocate for civil rights.

(6) **Walter Reuther** (1907–1970) was president of the United Automobile Workers (UAW) from 1946 until his death in 1970. Under his leadership, the UAW became one of the largest trade unions in the country, eventually growing to 1.5 million members. Reuther and the UAW were advocates of liberal reform and social justice. A skilled negotiator, Reuther won many work, medical, and retirement benefits for his union's members.

(7) **Floyd McKissick** (1922–1991) represented the Congress of Racial Equality (CORE) at the march. He read James Farmer's speech because Farmer, the president of CORE, had been arrested during a protest in Louisiana. McKissick was the first African American student at the University of North Carolina at Chapel Hill.

(8) **Rabbi Uri Miller** (1905–1972), the President of the American Jewish Congress, delivered a prayer.

(9) **Whitney Young Jr.** (1921–1971) led the National Urban League for a decade, beginning in 1961.

(10) **Mathew Ahmann** (1931–2001) was a founder and director of the National Catholic Conference.

(11) **Roy Wilkins** (1901–1981) was closely involved with the National Association for the Advancement of Colored People (NAACP) from the 1930s into the 1970s and was the executive director from 1955–1977. He helped grow participation in the NAACP from 50,000 to almost 400,000. He was wary of the more militant factions like the Black Power movement.

(12) **Rabbi Joachim Prinz** (1902–1988) served as president of the American Jewish Congress.

(13) **Dr. Martin Luther King Jr**. (1929–1968) was the president of the Southern Christian Leadership Conference.

"It's terrible to be circling up there without a place to land." Hansen, Drew D. *The Dream: Martin Luther King, Jr., and the Speech That Inspired a Nation.* New York: Ecco, 2003, p. 97.

"You have to preach," said Reverend Ralph Abernathy. *"Most of the folks coming tomorrow are coming to hear you preach."* Jones, Clarence B., and Stuart Connelly. *Behind the Dream: The Making of the Speech That Transformed a Nation.* New York: Palgrave Macmillan, 2011, p. 60.

Wyatt Tee Walker agreed, but added, *"Don't use the lines about 'I have a dream.' You have used it too many times already."* Younge, Gary. *The Speech: The Story Behind Dr. Martin Luther King Jr.'s Dream.* Chicago: Haymarket Books, 2013, p. 1.

Reverend Walter Fauntroy agreed. *"Whatever you do,"* he said, *"keep that in there."* Hansen, p. 66.

"I am now going upstairs to my room to counsel with my Lord." Jones and Connelly, p. 80.

"Until tomorrow, then," they mumbled. Ibid.

"It was like poetry," said Andrew Young. Hansen, p. 69.

"Tell them about the dream, Martin!" Jones and Connelly, p. 115.

"My country 'tis of thee" and *"Let freedom ring."* From "America," a patriotic hymn written by Samuel F. Smith in 1832.

"Let freedom ring" Hansen, pp. 108–109. From a speech by Chicago preacher and political activist, Archibald Carey, at the 1952 Republican National Convention.

"Free at last! Free at last! Thank God Almighty, we are free at last!" From "Free at Last" spiritual. The earliest example of this song (1907) was documented by African American collector John Wesley Work Jr. (also known as J. W. Work, I).

but saving a special welcome for Martin: "I have a dream." Euchner, Charles C. *Nobody Turn Me Around: A People's History of the 1963 March on Washington.* Boston: Beacon, 2010, p. 208.

"Leader, you swept today," Reverend Abernathy told Martin. Hansen, p. 169.

"You preached today," John Lewis added. Hansen, p. 170.

"You was smoking," Clarence Jones had told Martin moments after the speech. *"The words were so hot they was just burning off the page."* Hansen, p. 168.

Martin stepped up to the lectern, and stepped down on the other side of history. Jones, p. 124.

Bibliography

Bass, Patrik Henry. *Like a Mighty Stream: The March on Washington, August 28, 1963*. Philadelphia: Running Press, 2002.

Branch, Taylor. *Parting the Waters: America in the King Years, 1954–63*. New York: Simon and Schuster, 1988.

Hansen, Drew D. *The Dream: Martin Luther King, Jr., and the Speech That Inspired a Nation*. New York: Ecco, 2003.

Euchner, Charles. *Nobody Turn Me Around: A People's History of the 1963 March on Washington*. Boston: Beacon Press, 2010.

Jones, Clarence B., and Stuart Connelly. *Behind the Dream: The Making of the Speech That Transformed a Nation*. New York: Palgrave Macmillan, 2011.

King, Martin Luther, and Clayborne Carson. *The Autobiography of Martin Luther King, Jr.* New York: Intellectual Properties Management in Association with Warner Books, 1998.

Miller, W. Jason. *Origins of the Dream: Hughes's Poetry and King's Rhetoric*. Gainesville: University Press of Florida, 2015.

Williams, Juan. *Eyes on the Prize: America's Civil Rights Years, 1954–1965*. New York: Penguin Books, 2013.

Younge, Gary. *The Speech: The Story Behind Dr. Martin Luther King Jr.'s Dream*. Chicago: Haymarket Books, 2013.

In memory of Robert Solomon —B.W.

To the legacy of Martin Luther King Jr. and all who dare to dream his dream. —J.P.

Neal Porter Books

Text copyright © 2019 by Barry Wittenstein
Illustrations copyright © 2019 by Jerry Pinkney
All Rights Reserved
HOLIDAY HOUSE is registered in the U.S. Patent and Trademark Office.
Printed and bound in March 2019 at Toppan Leefung, DongGuan City, China.
The artwork for this book was made using graphite, color pencil, watercolor and collage on Arches watercolor paper
Book design by Jennifer Browne
www.holidayhouse.com
First Edition
10 9 8 7 6 5 4 3 2 1
The illustration on pp. 32-33 is after a photograph © Leonard Freed/Magnum Photos, www.magnumphotos.com.

Library of Congress Cataloging-in-Publication Data

Names: Wittenstein, Barry, author. | Pinkney, Jerry, illustrator.
Title: A place to land / Barry Wittenstein ; illustrated by Jerry Pinkney.
Description: New York : Holiday House, [2019] | "Neal Porter Books."
   Audience: Grades K–3. | Audience: Ages 6–9.
Identifiers: LCCN 2018042407 | ISBN 9780823443314 (hardcover)
Subjects: LCSH: King, Martin Luther, Jr., 1929–1968. I have a dream—
Juvenile literature. | Speeches, addresses, etc., American—Washington
(D.C.)—Juvenile literature. | March on Washington for Jobs and Freedom
(1963 : Washington, D.C.)—Juvenile literature. | African
Americans—Civil rights—History—20th century—Juvenile literature. | Civil rights
movements—United States—History—20th century—Juvenile literature.
Classification: LCC E185.97.K5 W588 2019 | DDC 323.092—dc23
LC record available at https://lccn.loc.gov/2018042407